Lyrics of Sunshine and Shadow

Lyrics of
Sunshine and Shadow

By

Paul Laurence Dunbar

New York
Dodd, Mead & Company
1905

Reprinted by Mnemosyne Publishing Co., Inc. Miami, Florida

First Mnemosyne reprinting 1969

Reprinted from a copy in the
Fisk University Library Negro Collection.

Copyright © 1969   Mnemosyne Publishing Co., Inc.   Miami, Florida

Library of Congress Catalog Card Number:
70-83919

Printed in the United States of America

TO MRS. FRANK CONOVER
WITH THANKS FOR HER
LONG BELIEF

CONTENTS

Contents

Contents

Contents

Lyrics of Sunshine and Shadow

Lyrics of Sunshine and Shadow

✿

A BOY'S SUMMER SONG

'TIS fine to play
    In the fragrant hay,
And romp on the golden load;
    To ride old Jack
    To the barn and back,
Or tramp by a shady road.
    To pause and drink,
    At a mossy brink;
Ah, that is the best of joy,
    And so I say
    On a summer's day,
What's so fine as being a boy? Ha, Ha!

    With line and hook
    By a babbling brook,
The fisherman's sport we ply;
    And list the song
    Of the feathered throng
That flit in the branches nigh.

Lyrics of Sunshine and Shadow

At last we strip
For a quiet dip;
Ah, that is the best of joy.
For this I say
On a summer's day,
What's so fine as being a boy? Ha, Ha!

THE SAND-MAN

I KNOW a man
With face of tan,
But who is ever kind;
Whom girls and boys
Leave games and toys
Each eventide to find.

When day grows dim,
They watch for him,
He comes to place his claim;
He wears the crown
Of Dreaming-town;
The sand-man is his name.

Lyrics of Sunshine and Shadow

When sparkling eyes
Droop sleepywise
And busy lips grow dumb;
When little heads
Nod toward the beds,
We know the sand-man's come.

JOHNNY SPEAKS

THE sand-man he's a jolly old fellow,
His face is kind and his voice is
mellow,
But he makes your eyelids as heavy as lead,
And then you got to go off to bed;
I don't think I like the sand-man.

But I've been playing this livelong day;
It does make a fellow so tired to play!
Oh, my, I'm a-yawning right here before
ma,
I'm the sleepiest fellow that ever you saw.
I think I do like the sand-man.

3

WINTER SONG

OH, who would be sad tho' the sky
    be a-graying,
  And meadow and woodlands are empty
    and bare;
For softly and merrily now there come
    playing,
  The little white birds thro' the winter-
    kissed air.

The squirrel's enjoying the rest of the
    thrifty,
  He munches his store in the old hollow
    tree;
Tho' cold is the blast and the snow-flakes
    are drifty
  He fears the white flock not a whit
    more than we.

4

Lyrics of Sunshine and Shadow

Chorus:

Then heigho for the flying snow!
Over the whitened roads we go,
    With pulses that tingle,
  .   And sleigh-bells a-jingle
For winter's white birds here's a cheery
  heigho!

A CHRISTMAS FOLKSONG

DE win' is blowin' wahmah,
    An hit's blowin' f'om de bay;
Dey's a so't o' mist a-risin'
  All erlong de meddah way;
Dey ain't a hint o' frostin'
  On de groun' ner in de sky,
An' dey ain't no use in hopin'
  Dat de snow'll 'mence to fly.
    It's goin' to be a green Christmas,
      An' sad de day fu' me.
    I wish dis was de las' one
      Dat evah I should see.

5

Lyrics of Sunshine and Shadow

Dey's dancin' in de cabin,
  Dey's spahkin' by de tree;
But dancin' times an' spahkin'
  Are all done pas' fur me.
Dey's feastin' in de big house,
  Wid all de windahs wide—
Is dat de way fu' people
  To meet de Christmas-tide?
    It's goin' to be a green Christmas,
      No mattah what you say.
    Dey's us dat will remembah
      An' grieve de comin' day.

Dey's des a bref o' dampness
  A-clingin' to my cheek;
De aih's been dahk an' heavy
  An' threatenin' fu' a week,
But not wid signs o' wintah,
  Dough wintah'd seem so deah—
De wintah's out o' season,
  An' Christmas eve is heah.
    It's goin' to be a green Christmas,
      An' oh, how sad de day!

Lyrics of Sunshine and Shadow

Go ax de hongry chu'chya'd,
   An' see what hit will say.

Dey's Allen on de hillside,
   An' Marfy in de plain;
Fu' Christmas was like springtime,
   An' come wid sun an' rain.
Dey's Ca'line, John, an' Susie,
   Wid only dis one lef':
An' now de curse is comin'
   Wid murder in hits bref.
      It's goin' to be a green Christmas—
         Des hyeah my words an' see:
      Befo' de summah beckons
         Dey's many'll weep wid me.

THE FOREST GREETING

GOOD hunting!—aye, good hunting,
   Wherever the forests call;
But ever a heart beats hot with fear,
And what of the birds that fall?

7

Lyrics of Sunshine and Shadow

Good hunting!—aye, good hunting,
   Wherever the north winds blow;
But what of the stag that calls for his mate?
   And what of the wounded doe?

Good hunting!—aye, good hunting,
   And ah! we are bold and strong;
But our triumph call through the forest hall
   Is a brother's funeral song.

For we are brothers ever,
   Panther and bird and bear;
Man and the weakest that fear his face,
   Born to the nest or lair.

Yes, brothers, and who shall judge us?
   Hunters and game are we;
But who gave the right for me to smite?
   Who boasts when he smiteth me?

Good hunting!—aye, good hunting,
   And dim is the forest track;
But the sportsman Death comes striding on:
   Brothers, the way is black.

Lyrics of Sunshine and Shadow

THE LILY OF THE VALLEY

SWEETEST of the flowers a-blooming
In the fragrant vernal days
Is the Lily of the Valley
With its soft, retiring ways.

Well, you chose this humble blossom
As the nurse's emblem flower,
Who grows more like her ideal
Every day and every hour.

Like the Lily of the Valley
In her honesty and worth,
Ah, she blooms in truth and virtue
In the quiet nooks of earth.

Tho' she stands erect in honor
When the heart of mankind bleeds,
Still she hides her own deserving
In the beauty of her deeds.

9

Lyrics of Sunshine and Shadow

In the silence of the darkness
  Where no eye may see and know,
There her footsteps shod with mercy,
  And fleet kindness come and go.

Not amid the sounds of plaudits,
  Nor before the garish day,
Does she shed her soul's sweet perfume,
  Does she take her gentle way.

But alike her ideal flower,
  With its honey-laden breath,
Still her heart blooms forth its beauty
  In the valley shades of death.

ENCOURAGED

BECAUSE you love me I have much
      achieved,
Had you despised me then I must have failed,
  But since I knew you trusted and believed,
I could not disappoint you and so prevailed.

Lyrics of Sunshine and Shadow

TO J. Q.

WHAT are the things that make
     life bright?
  A star gleam in the night.
What hearts us for the coming fray?
  The dawn tints of the day.
What helps to speed the weary mile?
  A brother's friendly smile.
What turns o' gold the evening gray?
  A flower beside the way.

DIPLOMACY

TELL your love where the roses
     blow,
  And the hearts of the lilies quiver,
Not in the city's gleam and glow,
  But down by a half-sunned river.

Lyrics of Sunshine and Shadow

Not in the crowded ball-room's glare,
　　That would be fatal, Marie, Marie,
How can she answer you then and there?
　　So come then and stroll with me,
　　　　my dear,
　　Down where the birds call, Marie,
　　Marie.

SCAMP

AIN'T it nice to have a mammy
　　W'en you kin' o' tiahed out
Wid a-playin' in de meddah,
　　An' a-runnin' roun' about
Till hit's made you mighty hongry,
　　An' yo' nose hit gits to know
What de smell means dat's a-comin'
　　F'om de open cabin do'?
　　　　She wash yo' face,
　　　　An' mek yo' place,
　　You's hongry as a tramp;
Den hit's eat you suppah right away,
　　You sta'vin' little scamp.

Lyrics of Sunshine and Shadow

W'en you's full o' braid an' bacon,
   An' dey ain't no mo' to eat,
An' de lasses dat's a-stickin'
   On yo' face ta'se kin' o' sweet,
Don' you t'ink hit's kin' o' pleasin'
   Fu' to have som'body neah
Dat'll wipe yo' han's an' kiss you
   Fo' dey lif' you f'om yo cheah?
     To smile so sweet,
     An' wash yo' feet,
   An' leave 'em co'l an' damp;
Den hit's come let me undress you, now
   You lazy little scamp.

Don' yo' eyes git awful heavy,
   An' yo' lip git awful slack,
Ain't dey som'p'n' kin' o' weaknin'
   In de backbone of yo' back?
Don' yo' knees feel kin' o' trimbly,
   An' yo' head go bobbin' roun',
W'en you says yo' " Now I lay me,"
   An' is sno'in' on de " down "?

13

She kiss yo' nose,
She kiss yo' toes,
An' den tu'n out de lamp,
Den hit's creep into yo' trunnel baid,
You sleepy little scamp.

WADIN' IN DE CRICK

DAYS git wa'm an' wa'mah,
    School gits mighty dull,
Seems lak dese hyeah teachahs
    Mus' feel mussiful.
Hookey's wrong, I know it
    Ain't no gent'man's trick;
But de aih's a-callin',
    "Come on to de crick."

Dah de watah's gu'glin'
    Ovah shiny stones,
Des hit's ve'y singin'
    Seems to soothe yo' bones.

14

Lyrics of Sunshine and Shadow

W'at's de use o' waitin',
    Go on good an' quick:
Dain't no fun lak dis hyeah
    Wadin' in de crick.

W'at dat jay-b'ud sayin'?
    Bettah shet yo' haid,
Fus' t'ing dat you fin' out,
    You'll be layin' daid.
Jay-bu'ds sich a tattlah,
    Des seem lak his trick
Fu' to tell on folkses
    Wadin' in de crick.

Willer boughs a-bendin',
    Hidin' of de sky,
Wavin' kin' o' frien'ly
    Ez de win' go by,
Elum trees a-shinin',
    Dahk an' green an' thick,
Seem to say, " I see yo'
    Wadin' in de crick."

Lyrics of Sunshine and Shadow

But de trees don' chattah,
    Dey des look an' sigh
Lak hit's kin' o' peaceful
    Des a-bein' nigh,
An' yo' t'ank yo' Mastah
    Dat dey trunks is thick
W'en yo' mammy fin's you
    Wadin' in de crick.

Den yo' run behin' dem
    Lak yo' scaihed to def,
Mammy come a-flyin',
    Mos' nigh out o' bref;
But she set down gentle
    An' she drap huh stick,—
An, fus' t'ing, dey's mammy
    Wadin' in de crick.

A CORN SONG

ON the wide veranda white,
    In the purple failing light,
Sits the master while the sun is lowly
    burning;

16

Lyrics of Sunshine and Shadow

And his dreamy thoughts are drowned
In the softly flowing sound
Of the corn-songs of the field hands slow
    returning.

Oh, we hoe de co'n
Since de ehly mo'n;
Now de sinkin' sun
Says de day is done.

O'er the fields with heavy tread,
Light of heart and high of head,
Though the halting steps be labored, slow,
    and weary;
Still the spirits brave and strong
Find a comforter in song,
And their corn-song rises ever loud and
    cheery.

Oh, we hoe de co'n
Since de ehly mo'n;
Now de sinkin' sun
Says de day is done.

17

Lyrics of Sunshine and Shadow

To the master in his seat,
Comes the burden, full and sweet,
Of the mellow minor music growing
    clearer,
As the toilers raise the hymn,
Thro' the silence dusk and dim,
To the cabin's restful shelter drawing
    nearer.

        Oh, we hoe de co'n
        Since de ehly mo'n;
        Now de sinkin' sun
        Says de day is done.

And a tear is in the eye
Of the master sitting by,
As he listens to the echoes low-replying
    To the music's fading calls
    As it faints away and falls
Into silence, deep within the cabin dying.

        Oh, we hoe de co'n
        Since de ehly mo'n;
        Now de sinkin' sun
        Says de day is done.

18

Lyrics of Sunshine and Shadow

THE PLANTATION CHILD'S LULLABY

WINTAH time hit comin'
    Stealin' thoo de night;
Wake up in the mo'nin'
    Evah ting is white;
Cabin lookin' lonesome
    Stannin' in de snow,
Meks you kin' o' nervous,
    W'en de win' hit blow.

Trompin' back from feedin',
    Col' an' wet an' blue,
Homespun jacket ragged,
    Win' a-blowin' thoo.
Cabin lookin' cheerful,
    Unnerneaf de do',
Yet you kin' o' keerful
    W'en de win' hit blow.

Lyrics of Sunshine and Shadow

Hickory log a-blazin'
  Light a-lookin' red,
Faith o' eyes o' peepin'
  R'om a trun'le bed,
Little feet a-patterin'
  Cleak across de flo';
Bettah had be keerful
  W'en de win' hit blow.

Suppah done an' ovah,
  Evah t'ing is still;
Listen to de snowman
  Slippin' down de hill.
Ashes on de fiah,
  Keep it wa'm but low.
What's de use o' keerin'
  Ef de win' do blow?

Smoke house full o' bacon,
  Brown an' sweet an' good;
Taters in de cellah,
  'Possum roam de wood;

Lyrics of Sunshine and Shadow

Little baby snoozin'
    Des ez ef he know.
What's de use o' keerin'
    Ef de win' do blow?

TWILIGHT

'TWIXT a smile and a tear,
    'Twixt a song and a sigh,
'Twixt the day and the dark,
    When the night draweth nigh.

Ah, sunshine may fade
    From the heavens above,
No twilight have we
    To the day of our love.

CURIOSITY

MAMMY'S in de kitchen, an' de do' is
    shet;
All de pickaninnies climb an' tug an' sweat,
Gittin' to de winder, stickin' dah lak flies,
Evah one ermong us des all nose an' eyes.

21

Lyrics of Sunshine and Shadow

" Whut's she cookin', Isaac? "   " Whut's
    she cookin', Jake? "
" Is it sweet pertaters?   Is hit pie er cake? "
But we couldn't mek out even whah we
    stood
Whut was mammy cookin' dat could smell
    so good.

Mammy spread de winder, an' she frown
    an' frown.
How de pickaninnies come a-tumblin' down!
Den she say: " Ef you-all keeps a-peepin' in,
How I'se gwine to whup you, my! 't 'ill
    be a sin!
Need n' come a-sniffin' an' a-nosin' hyeah,
'Ca'se I knows my business, nevah feah."
Won't somebody tell us—how I wish dey
    would!—
Whut is mammy cookin' dat it smells so
    good?

We know she means business, an' we
    dassent stay,
Dough it's mighty tryin' fuh to go erway;

But we goes a-troopin' down de ol' wood-
   track
'Twell dat steamin' kitchen brings us
   stealin' back,
Climbin' an' a-peepin' so's to see inside.
Whut on earf kin mammy be so sha'p to
   hide?
I'd des up an' tell folks w'en I knowed
   I could,
Ef I was a-cookin' t'ings dat smelt so good.

Mammy in de oven, an' I see huh smile;
Moufs mus' be a-wat'rin' roun' hyeah fuh
   a mile;
Den we almos' hollah ez we hu'ies down,
'Ca'se hit's apple dumplin's, big an' fat an'
   brown!
W'en de do' is opened, solemn lak an' slow,
Wisht you see us settin' all dah in a row
Innercent an' p'opah, des lak chillun should
W'en dey mammy's cookin' t'ings dat
   smell so good.

OPPORTUNITY

G RANNY'S gone a-visitin',
  Seen huh git huh shawl
W'en I was a-hidin' down
  Hime de gyahden wall.
Seen huh put her bonnet on,
  Seen huh tie de strings,
An' I'se gone to dreamin' now
  'Bout dem cakes an' t'ings.

On de she'f behime de do'—
  Mussy, what a feas'!
Soon ez she gits out o' sight,
  I kin eat in peace.
I bin watchin' fu' a week
  Des fu' dis hyeah chance.
Mussy, w'en I gits in daih,
  I'll des sholy dance.

Lyrics of Sunshine and Shadow

Lemon pie an' gingah-cake,
  Let me set an' t'ink—
Vinegah an' sugah, too,
  Dat 'll mek a drink;
Ef dey's one t'ing dat I loves
  Mos' pu'ticlahly,
It is eatin' sweet t'ings an'
  A-drinkin' Sangaree.

Lawdy, won' po' granny raih
  W'en she see de she'f;
W'en I t'ink erbout huh face,
  I's mos' 'shamed myse'f.
Well, she gone, an' hyeah I is,
  Back behime de do'—
Look hyeah! gran' 's done 'spected me,
  Dain't no sweets no mo'.

Evah sweet is hid erway,
  Job des done up brown;
Pusson t'ink dat someun t'ought
  Dey was t'eves erroun';
Dat des breaks my heart in two,
  Oh how bad I feel!

Des to t'ink my own gramma
B'lieved dat I 'u'd steal!

PUTTIN' THE BABY AWAY

EIGHT of 'em hyeah all tol' an' yet
   Dese eyes o' mine is wringin' wet;
My haht's a-achin' ha'd an' so',
De way hit nevah ached befo';
My soul's a-pleadin', " Lawd give back
Dis little lonesome baby black,
Dis one, dis las' po' he'pless one
Whose little race was too soon run."

Po' Little Jim, des fo' yeahs' ol'
A-layin' down so still an' col'.
Somehow hit don' seem ha'dly faih,
To have my baby lyin' daih
Wi'dout a smile upon his face,
Wi'dout a look erbout de place;
He ust to be so full o' fun
Hit don' seem right dat all's done, done.

Lyrics of Sunshine and Shadow

Des eight in all but I don' caih,
Dey wa'nt a single one to spaih;
De worl' was big, so was hy haht,
An' dis hyeah baby owned hit's paht;
De house was po', dey clothes was rough,
But daih was meat an' meal enough;
An' daih was room fu' little Jim;
Oh! Lawd, what made you call fu' him?

It do seem monst'ous ha'd to-day,
To lay dis baby boy away;
I'd learned to love his teasin' smile,
He mought o' des been lef' erwhile;
You wouldn't t'ought wid all de folks,
Dat's roun' hyeah mixin' teahs an' jokes,
De Lawd u'd had de time to see
Dis chile an' tek him 'way f'om me.

But let it go, I reckon Jim,
'll des go right straight up to Him
Dat took him f'om his mammy's nest
An' lef' dis achin' in my breas',
An' lookin' in dat fathah's face
An' 'memberin' dis lone sorrerin' place,

He'll say, " Good Lawd, you ought to had
Do sumpin' fu' to comfo't dad! "

THE FISHER CHILD'S LULLABY

THE wind is out in its rage to-night,
　　And your father is far at sea.
The rime on the window is hard and white
　But dear, you are near to me.
　　　Heave ho, weave low,
　　　　Waves of the briny deep;
　　　Seethe low and breathe low,
　　　　But sleep you, my little one,
　　　　　sleep, sleep.

The little boat rocks in the cove no more,
　But the flying sea-gulls wail;
I peer through the darkness that wraps
　　the shore,
　For sight of a home set sail.
　　Heave ho, weave low,

Waves of the briny deep;
Seethe low and breathe low,
But sleep you, my little one,
sleep, sleep.

Ay, lad of mine, thy father may die
In the gale that rides the sea,
But we'll not believe it, not you and I,
Who mind us of Galilee.
Heave ho, weave low,
Waves of the briny deep;
Seethe low and breathe low,
But sleep you, my little one,
sleep, sleep.

FAITH

I'S a-gittin' weary of de way dat people do,
De folks dat's got dey 'ligion in dey fiah-
place an' flue;
Dey's allus somep'n comin' so de spit'll have
to turn,

29

An' hit tain't no p'oposition fu' to mek de
hickory bu'n.
Ef de sweet pertater fails us an' de go'geous
yallah yam,
We kin tek a bit o' comfo't f'om ouah sto'
o' summah jam.
W'en de snow hit git to flyin', dat's de Mas-
tah's own desiah,
De Lawd'll run de wintah an' yo' mammy'll
run de fiah.

I ain' skeered because de win' hit staht to raih
and blow,
I ain't bothahed w'en he come er rattlin' at
de do',
Let him taih hisse'f an' shout, let him blow an'
bawl,

Dat's de time de branches shek an' bresh-wood
'mence to fall.
W'en de sto'm er railin' an' de shettahs blowin'
'bout,
Dat de time de fiah-place crack hits welcome
out.

Lyrics of Sunshine and Shadow

Tain' my livin' business fu' to trouble ner
    enquiah,
De Lawd'll min' de wintah an' my mammy'll
    min' de fiah.

Ash-cake allus gits ez brown w'en February's
    hyeah
Ez it does in bakin' any othah time o' yeah.
De bacon smell ez callin'-like, de kittle rock
    an' sing,
De same way in de wintah dat dey do it in de
    spring;
Dey ain't no use in mopin' 'round an' lookin'
    mad an' glum
Erbout de wintah season, fu' hit's des plumb
    boun' to come;

An' ef it comes to runnin' t'ings I's willin' to
    retiah,
De Lawd'll min' de wintah an' my mammy'll
    min' de fiah.

31

THE FARM CHILD'S LULLABY

OH, the little bird is rocking in the cradle
    of the wind,
  And it's bye, my little wee one, bye;
The harvest all is gathered and the pippins all
    are binned;
  Bye, my little wee one, bye;
The little rabbit's hiding in the golden shock
    of corn,
The thrifty squirrel's laughing bunny's idleness
    to scorn;
You are smiling with the angels in your slum-
    ber, smile till morn;
  So it's bye, my little wee one, bye.

There'll be plenty in the cellar, there'll be
    plenty on the shelf;
  Bye, my little wee one, bye;
There'll be goodly store of sweetings for a
    dainty little elf;
  Bye, my little wee one, bye.

Lyrics of Sunshine and Shadow

The snow may be a-flying o'er the meadow and
the hill,
The ice has checked the chatter of the little
laughing rill,
But in your cosey cradle you are warm and
happy still;
So bye, my little wee one, bye.

Why, the Bob White thinks the snowflake is a
brother to his song;
Bye, my little wee one, bye;
And the chimney sings the sweeter when the
wind is blowing strong;
Bye, my little wee one, bye;
The granary's overflowing, full is cellar, crib,
and bin,
The wood has paid its tribute and the ax has
ceased its din;
The winter may not harm you when you're
sheltered safe within;
So bye, my little wee one, bye.

Lyrics of Sunshine and Shadow

THE PLACE WHERE THE RAINBOW
ENDS

THERE'S a fabulous story
　　Full of splendor and glory,
　That Arabian legends transcends;
Of the wealth without measure,
The coffers of treasure,
　　At the place where the rainbow ends.

Oh, many have sought it,
And all would have bought it,
　With the blood we so recklessly
　　　spend;
But none has uncovered,
The gold, nor discovered
　The spot at the rainbow's end.

They have sought it in battle,
And e'en where the rattle
　Of dice with man's blasphemy
　　blends;

34

Lyrics of Sunshine and Shadow

But howe'er persuasive,
It still proves evasive,
   This place where the rainbow ends.

I own for my pleasure,
I yearn not for treasure,
   Though gold has a power it lends;
And I have a notion,
To find without motion,
   The place where the rainbow ends.

The pot may hold pottage,
The place be a cottage,
   That a humble contentment defends,
Only joy fills its coffer,
But spite of the scoffer,
   There's the place where the rainbow
     ends.

Where care shall be quiet,
And love shall run riot,
   And I shall find wealth in my
     friends;

Then truce to the story,
Of riches and glory;
    There's the place where the rainbow
    ends.

HOPE

DE dog go howlin' 'long de road,
    De night come shiverin' down;
My back is tiahed of its load,
    I cain't be fu' f'om town.
No mattah ef de way is long,
My haht is swellin' wid a song,
    No mattah 'bout de frownin' skies,
    I'll soon be home to see my Lize.

My shadder staggah on de way,
    It's monstous col' to-night;
But I kin hyeah my honey say
    " W'y bless me if de sight

O' you ain't good fu' my so' eyes."
(Dat talk's dis lak my lady Lize)
  I's so'y case de way was long
  But Lawd you bring me love an' song.

No mattah ef de way is long,
  An' ef I trimbles so'
I knows de fiah's burnin' strong,
  Behime my Lizy's do'.
An' daih my res' an' joy shell be,
Whaih my ol' wife's awaitin' me—
  Why what I keer fu' stingin' blas',
  I see huh windah light at las'.

APPRECIATION

MY muvver's ist the nicest one
    'At ever lived wiz folks;
She lets you have ze mostes' fun,
  An' laffs at all your jokes.

Lyrics of Sunshine and Shadow

I got a ol' maid auntie, too,
  The worst you ever saw;
Her eyes ist bore you through and
    through,—
  She ain't a bit like ma.

She's ist as slim as slim can be,
  An' when you want to slide
Down on ze balusters, w'y she
  Says 'at she's harrified.

She ain't as nice as Uncle Ben,
  What says 'at little boys
Won't never grow to be big men
  Unless they're fond of noise.

But muvver's nicer zan 'em all,
  She calls you, " precious lamb,"
An' let's you roll your ten-pin ball,
  An' spreads your bread wiz jam.

An' when you're bad, she ist looks sad,
  You fink she's goin' to cry;
An' when she don't you're awful glad,
  An' den you're good, Oh, my!

Lyrics of Sunshine and Shadow

At night, she takes ze softest hand,
  An' lays it on your head,
An' says " Be off to Sleepy-Land
  By way o' trundle-bed."

So when you fink what muvver knows
  An' aunts an' uncle tan't,
It skeers a feller; ist suppose
  His muvver 'd been a aunt.

THE BARRIER

THE Midnight wooed the Morning Star,
  And prayed her: " Love come
    nearer;
Your swinging coldly there afar
  To me but makes you dearer."

The Morning Star was pale with dole
  As said she, low replying:
" Oh, lover mine, soul of my soul,
  For you I too am sighing."

" But One ordained when we were born,
  In spite of love's insistence,
That night might only view the Morn
  Adoring at a distance."

But as she spoke, the jealous Sun
  Across the heavens panted;
" Oh, whining fools," he cried, " have
    done,
  Your wishes shall be granted."

He hurled his flaming lances far;
  The twain stood unaffrighted,
And Midnight and the Morning Star
  Lay down in death united.

DAY

THE gray dawn on the mountain top
  Is slow to pass away.
Still lays him by in sluggish dreams,
  The golden God of day.

Lyrics of Sunshine and Shadow

And then a light along the hills,
  Your laughter silvery gay;
The Sun God wakes, a bluebird trills,
  You come and it is day.

TO DAN

STEP me now a bridal measure,
    Work give way to love and leisure,
Hearts be free and hearts be gay—
Doctor Dan doth wed to-day.

Diagnosis, cease your squalling—
Check that scalpel's senseless bawling,
Put that ugly knife away—
Doctor Dan doth wed to-day.

'Tis no time for things unsightly,
Life's the day and life goes lightly;
Science lays aside her sway–
Love rules Dr. Dan to-day.

Gather, gentlemen and ladies,
For the nuptial feast now made is,

Lyrics of Sunshine and Shadow

Swing your garlands, chant your lay
For the pair who wed to-day.

Wish them happy days and many,
Troubles few and griefs not any,
Lift your brimming cups and say
God bless them who wed to-day.

Then a cup to Cupid daring,
Who for conquest ever faring,
With his arrows dares assail
E'en a doctor's coat of mail.

So with blithe and happy hymning
And with harmless goblets brimming,
Dance a step—musicians play—
Doctor Dan doth wed to-day.

WHAT'S THE USE

WHAT'S the use o' folks
a-frownin'
When the way's a little rough?

Lyrics of Sunshine and Shadow

Frowns lay out the road fur smilin'
You'll be wrinkled soon enough.
What's the use?

What's the use o' folks a-sighin'?
It's an awful waste o' breath,
An' a body can't stand wastin'
What he needs so bad in death.
What's the use?

What's the use o' even weepin'?
Might as well go long an' smile.
Life, our longest, strongest arrow,
Only lasts a little while.
What's the use?

A LAZY DAY

THE trees bend down along the
stream,
Where anchored swings my tiny boat.
The day is one to drowse and dream
And list the thrush's throttling note.
When music from his bosom bleeds
Among the river's rustling reeds.

43

Lyrics of Sunshine and Shadow

No ripple stirs the placid pool,
   When my adventurous line is cast,
A truce to sport, while clear and cool,
   The mirrored clouds slide softly past.
The sky gives back a blue divine,
And all the world's wide wealth is mine.

A pickerel leaps, a bow of light,
The minnows shine from side to side.
The first faint breeze comes up the tide—
I pause with half uplifted oar,
While night drifts down to claim the shore.

ADVICE

W'EN you full o' worry
   'Bout yo' wo'k an' sich,
W'en you kind o' bothered
   Case you can't get rich,
An' yo' neighboh p'ospah
   Past his jest desu'ts,
An' de sneer of comerds
   Stuhes yo' heaht an' hu'ts,

44

Lyrics of Sunshine and Shadow

Des don' pet yo' worries,
   Lay 'em on de she'f,
Tek a little trouble
   Brothah, wid yo'se'f.

Ef a frien' comes mou'nin'
   'Bout his awful case,
You know you don' grieve him
   Wid a gloomy face,
But you wrassle wid him,
   Try to tek him in;
Dough hit cracks yo' features,
   Law, you smile lak sin,
Ain't you good ez he is?
   Don' you pine to def;
Tek a little trouble
   Brothah, wid yo'se'f.

Ef de chillun pestahs,
   An' de baby's bad,
Ef yo' wife gits narvous,
   An' you're gettin' mad,

45

Lyrics of Sunshine and Shadow

Des you grab yo' boot-strops,
  Hol' yo' body down,
Stop a-tinkin' cuss-w'rds,
  Chase away de frown,
Knock de haid o' worry,
  Twell dey ain' none lef';
Tek a little trouble,
  Brothah, wid yo'se'f.

LIMITATIONS

EF you's only got de powah fe' to blow a
    little whistle,
Keep ermong de people wid de whistles.
Ef you don't, you'll fin' out sho'tly dat you's
    th'owed yo' fines' feelin'
In a place dat's all a bed o' thistles.
'Tain't no use a-goin' now, ez sho's you bo'n,
A-squeakin' of yo' whistle 'g'inst a gread big
    ho'n.

Ef you ain't got but a teenchy bit o' victuals
    on de table,
  Whut' de use a-claimin' hit's a feas'?

Lyrics of Sunshine and Shadow

Fe' de folks is mighty 'spicious, an' dey's ap'
    to come a-peerin',
  Lookin' fe' de scraps you lef' at leas'.
W'en de meal's a-hidin' f'om de meal-bin's top,
You needn't talk to hide it; ef you sta'ts, des
    stop.

Ef yo' min' kin only carry half a pint o' com-
    mon idees,
  Don' go roun' a-sayin' hit's a bar'l;
'Ca'se de people gwine to test you, an' dey'll
    fin' out you's a-lyin',
  Den dey'll twis' yo' sayin's in a snarl.
Wuss t'ing in de country dat I evah hyahed—
A crow dot sat a-squawkin', "I's a mockin'-
    bird."

A GOLDEN DAY

I FOUND you and I lost you,
  All on a gleaming day.
The day was filled with sunshine,
  And the land was full of May.

47

A golden bird was singing
  Its melody divine,
I found you and I loved you,
  And all the world was mine.

I found you and I lost you,
  All on a golden day,
But when I dream of you, dear,
  It is always brimming May.

THE UNLUCKY APPLE

'TWAS the apple that in Eden
    Caused our father's primal
      fall;
And the Trojan War, remember—
  'Twas an apple caused it all.
So for weeks I've hesitated,
  You can guess the reason why,
For I want to tell my darling
  She's the apple of my eye.

Lyrics of Sunshine and Shadow

THE DISCOVERY

THESE are the days of elfs and fays:
    Who says that with the dreams of
       myth,
These imps and elves disport themselves?
Ah no, along the paths of song
Do all the tiny folk belong.

Round all our homes,
Kobolds and gnomes do daily cling,
Then nightly fling their lanterns out.
And shout on shout, they join the rout,
And sing, and sing, within the sweet enchanted
    ring.

Where gleamed the guile of moonlight's smile,
Once paused I, listening for a while,
And heard the lay, unknown by day,—
The fairies' dancing roundelay.

49

Lyrics of Sunshine and Shadow

Queen Mab was there, her shimmering hair
Each fairy prince's heart's despair.
She smiled to see their sparkling glee,
And once I ween, she smiled at me.

Since when, you may by night or day,
Dispute the sway of elf-folk gay;
But, hear me, stay!
I've learned the way to find Queen Mab and
    elf and fay.

Where e'er by streams, the moonlight gleams,
Or on a meadow softly beams,
There, footing round on dew-lit ground,
The fairy folk may all be found.

MORNING

THE mist has left the greening
    plain,
The dew-drops shine like fairy rain,
The coquette rose awakes again
    Her lovely self adorning.

Lyrics of Sunshine and Shadow

The Wind is hiding in the trees,
A sighing, soothing, laughing tease,
Until the rose says " Kiss me, please,"
   'Tis morning, 'tis morning.

With staff in hand and careless-free,
The wanderer fares right jauntily,
For towns and houses are, thinks he,
   For scorning, for scorning.
My soul is swift upon the wing,
And in its deeps a song I bring;
Come, Love, and we together sing,
   " 'Tis morning, 'tis morning."

THE AWAKENING

I DID not know that life could be so sweet,
   I did not know the hours could speed so
     fleet,
Till I knew you, and life was sweet again.
The days grew brief with love and lack of
     pain—

51

Lyrics of Sunshine and Shadow

I was a slave a few short days ago,
The powers of Kings and Princes now I know;
I would not be again in bondage, save
I had your smile, the liberty I crave.

LOVE'S DRAFT

THE draft of love was cool and sweet
    You gave me in the cup,
But, ah, love's fire is keen and fleet,
    And I am burning up.

Unless the tears I shed for you
    Shall quench this burning flame,
It will consume me through and through,
    And leave but ash—a name.

A MUSICAL

OUTSIDE the rain upon the
    street,
    The sky all grim of hue,
Inside, the music-painful sweet,
    And yet I heard but you.

Lyrics of Sunshine and Shadow

As is a thrilling violin,
  So is your voice to me,
And still above the other strains,
  It sang in ecstasy.

TWELL DE NIGHT IS PAS'

ALL de night long twell de moon goes
    down,
  Lovin' I set at huh feet,
Den fu' de long jou'ney back f'om de town,
  Ha'd, but de dreams mek it sweet.

All de night long twell de break of de day,
  Dreamin' agin in my sleep,
Mandy comes drivin' my sorrers away,
  Axin' me, " Wha' fu' you weep? "

All de day long twell de sun goes down,
  Smilin', I ben' to my hoe,
Fu' dough de weddah git nasty an' frown,
  One place I know I kin go.

53

All my life long twell de night has pas'
  Let de wo'k come ez it will,
So dat I fin' you, my honey, at las',
  Somewhaih des ovah de hill.

BLUE

STANDIN' at de winder,
    Feelin' kind o' glum,
Listenin' to de raindrops
    Play de kettle drum,
Lookin' crost de medders
    Swimmin' lak a sea;
Lawd 'a' mussy on us,
    What's de good o' me?

Can't go out a-hoein',
    Wouldn't ef I could;
Groun' too wet fu' huntin',
    Fishin' ain't no good.
Too much noise fo' sleepin',
    No one hyeah to chat;
Des mus' stan' an' listen
    To dat pit-a-pat.

Hills is gittin' misty,
    Valley's gittin' dahk;
Watch-dog's 'mence a-howlin',
    Rathah have 'em ba'k
Dan a-moanin' solemn
    Somewhaih out o' sight;
Rain-crow des a-chucklin'—
    Dis is his delight.

Mandy, bring my banjo,
    Bring de chillen in,
Come in f'om de kitchen,
    I feel sick ez sin.
Call in Uncle Isaac,
    Call Aunt Hannah, too,
Tain't no use in talkin',
    Chile, I's sholy blue.

DREAMIN' TOWN

COME away to dreamin' town,
    Mandy Lou, Mandy Lou,
Whaih de skies don' nevah frown,
    Mandy Lou;

Lyrics of Sunshine and Shadow

Whaih de streets is paved with gol',
Whaih de days is nevah col',
An' no sheep strays f'om de fol',
    Mandy Lou.

Ain't you tiahed of every day,
    Mandy Lou, Mandy Lou,
Tek my han' an' come away,
    Mandy Lou,
To the place whaih dreams is King,
Whaih my heart hol's everything,
An' my soul can allus sing,
    Mandy Lou.

Come away to dream wid me,
    Mandy Lou, Mandy Lou,
Whaih our hands an' hea'ts are free,
    Mandy Lou;
Whaih de sands is shinin' white,
Whaih de rivahs glistens bright,
    Mandy Lou.

Lyrics of Sunshine and Shadow

Come away to dreamland town,
  Mandy Lou, Mandy Lou,
Whaih de fruit is bendin' down,
  Des fu' you.
Smooth your brow of lovin' brown,
An' my love will be its crown;
Come away to dreamin' town,
        Mandy Lou.

AT NIGHT

WHUT time 'd dat clock strike?
    Nine? No—eight;
I didn't think hit was so late.
Aer chew! I must 'a' got a cough,
  I raally b'lieve I did doze off—
Hit's mighty soothin' to de tiah,
  A-dozin' dis way by de fiah;
Oo oom—hit feels so good to stretch
  I sutny is one weary wretch!

Look hyeah, dat boy done gone to sleep!
He des ain't wo'th his boa'd an' keep;

57

Lyrics of Sunshine and Shadow

I des don't b'lieve he'd bat his eyes
    If Gab'el called him fo'm de skies!
But sleepin's good dey ain't no doubt—
    Dis pipe o' mine is done gone out.
Don't bu'n a minute, bless my soul,
    Des please to han' me dat ah coal.

You 'Lias git up now, my son,
    Seems lak my nap is des begun;
You sutny mus' ma'k down de day
    W'en I treats comp'ny dis away!
W'y, Brother Jones, dat drowse come on,
    An' laws! I dremp dat you was gone!
You 'Lias, whaih yo' mannahs, suh,
    To hyeah me call an' nevah stuh!

To-morrer mo'nin' w'en I call
    Dat boy'll be sleepin' to beat all,
Don't mek no diffunce how I roah,
    He'll des lay up an' sno' and sno'.
Now boy, you done hyeahed whut I said,
    You bettah tek yo'se'f yo baid,
Case ef you gits me good an' wrong
    I'll mek dat sno' a diffunt song.

Lyrics of Sunshine and Shadow

Dis wood fiah is invitin' dho',
    Hit seems to wa'm de ve'y flo'—
An' nuffin' ain't a whit ez sweet,
    Ez settin' toastin' of yo' feet.
Hit mek you drowsy, too, but La!
    Hyeah, 'Lias, don't you hyeah yo' ma?
Ef I gits sta'ted f'om dis cheah
    I' lay, you scamp, I'll mek you heah!

To-morrer mo'nin' I kin bawl
    Twell all de neighbohs hyeah me call;
An' you'll be snoozin' des ez deep
    Ez if de day was made fu' sleep;
Hit's funny when you got a cough
    Somehow yo' voice seems too fu' off—
Can't wake dat boy fu' all I say,
    I reckon he'll sleep daih twell day!

KIDNAPED

I HELD my heart so far from harm,
    I let it wander far and free
In mead and mart, without alarm,
    Assured it must come back to me.

Lyrics of Sunshine and Shadow

And all went well till on a day,
  Learned Dr. Cupid wandered by
A search along our sylvan way
  For some peculiar butterfly.

A flash of wings, a hurried drive,
  A flutter and a short-lived flit;
This Scientist, as I am alive
  Had seen my heart and captured it.

Right tightly now 'tis held among
  The specimens that he has trapped,
And sings (Oh, love is ever young),
  'Tis passing sweet to be kidnaped.

COMPENSATION

BECAUSE I had loved so deeply,
  Because I had loved so long,
God in His great compassion
  Gave me the gift of song.

Lyrics of Sunshine and Shadow

Because I have loved so vainly,
    And sung with such faltering
        breath,
The Master in infinite mercy
    Offers the boon of Death.

WINTER'S APPROACH

DE sun hit shine an' de win' hit blow,
    Ol' Brer Rabbit be a-layin' low,
He know dat de wintah time a-comin',
De huntah man he walk an' wait,
He walk right by Brer Rabbit's gate—
    He know—

De dog he lick his sliverin' chop,
An' he tongue 'gin' his mouf go flop, flop—
    He—
He rub his nose fu' to clah his scent
So's to tell w'ich way dat cotton-tail went,
    He—

61

Lyrics of Sunshine and Shadow

De huntah's wife she set an' spin
A good wahm coat fu' to wrop him in
    She—
She look at de skillet an' she smile, oh my!
An' ol' Brer Rabbit got to sholy fly.
    Dey know.

ANCHORED

IF thro' the sea of night which here sur-
    rounds me,
  I could swim out beyond the farthest star,
Break every barrier of circumstance that
    bounds me,
  And greet the Sun of sweeter life afar,

Tho' near you there is passion, grief, and
    sorrow,
  And out there rest and joy and peace and all,
I should renounce that beckoning for to-
    morrow,
  I could not choose to go beyond your call.

Lyrics of Sunshine and Shadow

THE VETERAN

UNDERNEATH the autumn sky,
  Haltingly, the lines go by.
Ah, would steps were blithe and gay,
As when first they marched away,
Smile on lip and curl on brow,—
Only white-faced gray-beards now,
Standing on life's outer verge,
E'en the marches sound a dirge.

Blow, you bugles, play, you fife,
Rattle, drums, for dearest life.
Let the flags wave freely so,
As the marching legions go,
Shout, hurrah and laugh and jest,
This is memory at its best.
(Did you notice at your quip,
That old comrade's quivering lip?)

63

Lyrics of Sunshine and Shadow

Ah, I see them as they come,
Stumbling with the rumbling drum;
But a sight more sad to me
E'en than these ranks could be
Was that one with cane upraised
Who stood by and gazed and gazed,
Trembling, solemn, lips compressed,
Longing to be with the rest.

Did he dream of old alarms,
As he stood, "presented arms"?
Did he think of field and camp
And the unremitting tramp
Mile on mile—the lonely guard
When he kept his midnight ward?
Did he dream of wounds and scars
In that bitter war of wars?

What of that? He stood and stands
In my memory—trembling hands,
Whitened beard and cane and all
As if waiting for the call

Lyrics of Sunshine and Shadow

Once again: "To arms, my sons,"
And his ears hear far-off guns,
Roll of cannon and the tread
Of the legions of the Dead!

YESTERDAY AND TO-MORROW

YESTERDAY I held your hand,
    Reverently I pressed it,
And its gentle yieldingness
From my soul I blessed it.

But to-day I sit alone,
Sad and sore repining;
Must our gold forever know
Flames for the refining?

Yesterday I walked with you,
Could a day be sweeter?
Life was all a lyric song
Set to tricksy meter.

Lyrics of Sunshine and Shadow

Ah, to-day is like a dirge,—
Place my arms around you,
Let me feel the same dear joy
As when first I found you.

Let me once retrace my steps,
From these roads unpleasant,
Let my heart and mind and soul
All ignore the present.

Yesterday the iron seared
And to-day means sorrow.
Pause, my soul, arise, arise,
Look where gleams the morrow.

THE CHANGE

LOVE used to carry a bow, you know,
But now he carries a taper;
It is either a length of wax aglow,
Or a twist of lighted paper.

Lyrics of Sunshine and Shadow

I pondered a little about the scamp,
   And then I decided to follow
His wandering journey to field and
     camp,
   Up hill, down dale or hollow.

I dogged the rollicking, gay, young
     blade
   In every species of weather;
Till, leading me straight to the home of
     a maid
   He left us there together.

And then I saw it, oh, sweet surprise,
   The taper it set a-burning
The love-light brimming my lady's eyes,
   And my heart with the fire of
     yearning.

THE CHASE

THE wind told the little leaves to hurry,
    And chased them down the way,
While the mother tree laughed loud in glee,
    For she thought her babes at play.

The cruel wind and the rain laughed loudly,
    We'll bury them deep, they said,
And the old tree grieves, and the little leaves
    Lie low, all chilled and dead.

SUPPOSE

IF 'twere fair to suppose
    That your heart were not taken,
That the dew from the rose
    Petals still were not shaken,

Lyrics of Sunshine and Shadow

I should pluck you,
    Howe'er you should thorn me and
        scorn me,
And wear you for life as the green of
    the bower.

If 'twere fair to suppose
    That that road was for vagrants,
That the wind and the rose,
    Counted all in their fragrance;
Oh, my dear one,
    By love, I should take you and
        make you,
The green of my life from the
    scintillant hour.

THE DEATH OF THE FIRST BORN

COVER him over with daisies white,
    And eke with the poppies red,
Sit with me here by his couch to-night,
    For the First-Born, Love, is dead.

69

Lyrics of Sunshine and Shadow

Poor little fellow, he seemed so fair
    As he lay in my jealous arms;
Silent and cold he is lying there
    Stripped of his darling charms.

Lusty and strong he had grown
    forsooth,
    Sweet with an infinite grace,
Proud in the force of his conquering
    youth,
    Laughter alight in his face.

Oh, but the blast, it was cruel and
    keen,
    And ah, but the chill it was rare;
The look of the winter-kissed flow'r
    you've seen
    When meadows and fields were
    bare.

Can you not wake from this white,
    cold sleep
    And speak to me once again?

Lyrics of Sunshine and Shadow

True that your slumber is deep, so
    deep,
  But deeper by far is my pain.

Cover him over with daisies white,
  And eke with the poppies red,
Sit with me here by his couch to-night,
  For the First-Born, Love, is dead.

BEIN' BACK HOME

HOME agin, an' home to stay—
    Yes, it's nice to be away.
Plenty things to do an' see,
But the old place seems to me
Jest about the proper thing.
Mebbe 'ts 'cause the mem'ries cling
Closer 'round yore place o' birth
'N ary other spot on earth.

W'y it's nice jest settin' here,
Lookin' out an' seein' clear,
'Thout no smoke, ner dust, ner haze
In these sweet October days.

Lyrics of Sunshine and Shadow

What's as good as that there lane,
Kind o' browned from last night's
    rain?
'Pears like home has got the start
When the goal's a feller's heart.

What's as good as that there jay
Screechin' up'ards towards the gray
Skies? An' tell me, what's as fine
As that full-leafed pumpkin vine?
Tow'rin' buildin's—yes, they're good;
But in sight o' field and wood,
Then a feller understan's
'Bout the house not made with han's

Let the others rant an' roam
When they git away from home;
Jest gi' me my old settee
An' my pipe beneath a tree;
Sight o' medders green an' still,
Now and then a gentle hill,
Apple orchards, full o' fruit,
Nigh a cider press to boot—

Lyrics of Sunshine and Shadow

That's the thing jest done up brown;
D'want to be too nigh to town;
Want to have the smells an' sights,
An' the dreams o' long still nights,
With the friends you used to know
In the keerless long ago—
Same old cronies, same old folks,
Same old cider, same old jokes.

Say, it's nice a-gittin' back,
When yore pulse is growin' slack,
An' yore breath begins to wheeze
Like a fair-set valley breeze;
Kind o' nice to set aroun'
On the old familiar groun',
Knowin' that when Death does come,
That he'll find you right at home.

THE OLD CABIN

IN de dead of night I sometimes,
Git to t'inkin' of de pas'

Lyrics of Sunshine and Shadow

An' de days w'en slavery helt me
    In my mis'ry—ha'd an' fas'.
Dough de time was mighty tryin',
    In dese houahs somehow hit seem
Dat a brightah light come slippin'
    Thoo de kivahs of my dream.

An' my min' fu'gits de whuppins
    Draps de feah o' block an' lash
An' flies straight to somep'n' joyful
    In a secon's lightnin' flash.
Den hit seems I see a vision
    Of a dearah long ago
Of de childern tumblin' roun' me
    By my rough ol' cabin do'.

Talk about yo' go'geous mansions
    An' yo' big house great an' gran',
Des bring up de fines' palace
    Dat you know in all de lan'.
But dey's somep'n' dearah to me,
    Somep'n' faihah to my eyes
In dat cabin, less you bring me
    To yo' mansion in de skies.

Lyrics of Sunshine and Shadow

I kin see de light a-shinin'
  Thoo de chinks atween de logs,
I kin hyeah de way-off bayin'
  Of my mastah's huntin' dogs,
An' de neighin' of de hosses
  Stampin' on de ol' bahn flo',
But above dese soun's de laughin'
  At my deah ol' cabin do'.

We would gethah daih at evenin',
  All my frien's 'ud come erroun'
An' hit wan't no time, twell, bless you,
  You could hyeah de banjo's soun'.
You could see de dahkies dancin'
  Pigeon wing an' heel an' toe,—
Joyous times I tell you people
  Roun' dat same ol' cabin do'.

But at times my t'oughts gits saddah,
  Ez I riccolec' de folks,
An' dey frolickin' an' talkin'
  Wid dey laughin' an' dey jokes.
An' hit hu'ts me w'en I membahs
  Dat I'll nevah see no mo'

Dem ah faces gethered smilin'
Roun' dat po' ol' cabin do'.

DESPAIR

LET me close the eyes of my soul
    That I may not see
What stands between thee and me.

Let me shut the ears of my heart
    That I may not hear
A voice that drowns yours, my dear.

Let me cut the cords of my life,
    Of my desolate being,
Since cursed is my hearing and seeing.

CIRCUMSTANCES ALTER CASES

TIM Murphy's gon' walkin' wid Maggie
    O'Neill,
      O chone!
If I was her muther, I'd frown on sich foolin',
      O chone!

Lyrics of Sunshine and Shadow

I'm sure its unmutherlike, darin' an' wrong
To let a gyrul hear 'tell the sass an' the song
Of every young felly that happens along,
      O chone!

An' Murphy, the things that's be'n sed of his
    doin',
      O chone!
'Tis a cud that no dacent folks wants to be
    chewin',
      O chone!
If he came to my door wid his cane on a twirl,
Fur to thry to make love to you, Biddy, my
    girl,
Ah, wouldn't I send him away wid a whirl,
      O chone!

They say the gossoon is indecent and dirty,
      O chone!
In spite of his dressin' so.
      O chone!
Let him dress up ez foine ez a king or a queen,
Let him put on more wrinkles than ever was
    seen,

Lyrics of Sunshine and Shadow

You'll be sure he's no match for my little
colleen,
O chone!

Faith the two is comin' back an' their walk is
all over,
O chone!
'Twas a pretty short walk fur to take wid a
lover,
O chone!
Why, I believe that Tim Murphy's a kumin'
this way,
Ah, Biddy jest look at him steppin' so gay,
I'd niver belave what the gossipers say,
O chone!

He's turned in the gate an' he's coming a-
caperin',
O chone!
Go Biddy, go quick an' put on a clane apern,
O chone!

78

Lyrics of Sunshine and Shadow

Be quick as ye kin fur he's right at the dure;
Come in, master Tim, fur ye're welcome I'm
  shure.
We were talkin' o' ye jest a minute before.
        O chone!

TILL THE WIND GETS RIGHT

OH the breeze is blowin' balmy
    And the sun is in a haze;
There's a cloud jest givin' coolness,
    To the laziest of days.
There are crowds upon the lakeside,
    But the fish refuse to bite,
So I'll wait and go a-fishin'
    When the wind gets right.

Now my boat tugs at her anchor,
    Eager now to kiss the spray,
While the little waves are callin'
    Drowsy sailor come away,

79

Lyrics of Sunshine and Shadow

There's a harbor for the happy,
   And its sheen is just in sight,
But I won't set sail to get there,
   Till the wind gets right.

That's my trouble, too, I reckon,
   I've been waitin' all too long,
Tho' the days were always
   Still the wind is always wrong.
An' when Gabriel blows his trumpet,
   In the day o' in the night,
I will still be found waitin',
   Till the wind gets right.

A SUMMER NIGHT

SUMMAH is de lovin' time—
   Do' keer what you say.
Night is allus peart an' prime,
   Bettah dan de day.
Do de day is sweet an' good,
   Birds a-singin' fine,
Pines a-smellin' in de wood,—
   But de night is mine.

Lyrics of Sunshine and Shadow

Rivah whisperin' " howdy do,"
    Ez it pass you by—
Moon a-lookin' down at you,
    Winkin' on de sly.
Frogs a-croakin' f'om de pon',
    Singin' bass dey fill,
An' you listen way beyon'
    Ol' man whippo'will.

Hush up, honey, tek my han',
    Mek yo' footsteps light;
Somep'n' kin' o' hol's de lan'
    On a summah night.
Somep'n' dat you nevah sees
    An' you nevah hyeahs,
But you feels it in de breeze,
    Somep'n' nigh to teahs.

Somep'n' nigh to teahs? dat's so;
    But hit's nigh to smiles.
An' you feels it ez you go
    Down de shinin' miles,

Lyrics of Sunshine and Shadow

Tek my han', my little dove;
  Hush an' come erway—
Summah is de time fu' love,
  Night-time beats de day!

AT SUNSET TIME

A DOWN the west a golden glow
    Sinks burning in the sea,
And all the dreams of long ago
  Come flooding back to me.
The past has writ a story strange
  Upon my aching heart,
But time has wrought a subtle change,
  My wounds have ceased to smart.

No more the quick delight of youth,
  No more the sudden pain,
I look no more for trust or truth
  Where greed may compass gain.
What, was it I who bared my heart
  Through unrelenting years,
And knew the sting of misery's dart,
  The tang of sorrow's tears?

82

'Tis better now, I do not weep,
  I do not laugh nor care;
My soul and spirit half asleep
  Drift aimless everywhere.
We float upon a sluggish stream,
  We ride no rapids mad,
While life is all a tempered dream
  And every joy half sad.

NIGHT

SILENCE, and whirling worlds afar
    Through all encircling skies.
What floods come o'er the spirit's bar,
  What wondrous thoughts arise.

The earth, a mantle falls away,
  And, winged, we leave the sod;
Where shines in its eternal sway
  The majesty of God.

AT LOAFING-HOLT

SINCE I left the city's heat
For this sylvan, cool retreat,
High upon the hill-side here
Where the air is clean and clear,
I have lost the urban ways.
Mine are calm and tranquil days,
Sloping lawns of green are mine,
Clustered treasures of the vine;
Long forgotten plants I know,
Where the best wild berries grow,
Where the greens and grasses sprout,
When the elders blossom out.
Now I am grown weather-wise
With the lore of winds and skies.
Mine the song whose soft refrain
Is the sigh of summer rain.
Seek you where the woods are cool,
Would you know the shady pool

84

Lyrics of Sunshine and Shadow

Where, throughout the lazy day,
Speckled beauties drowse or play?
Would you find in rest or peace
Sorrow's permanent release?—
Leave the city, grim and gray,
Come with me, ah, come away.
Do you fear the winter chill,
Deeps of snow upon the hill?
'Tis a mantle, kind and warm,
Shielding tender shoots from harm.
Do you dread the ice-clad streams,—
They are mirrors for your dreams.
Here's a rouse, when summer's past
To the raging winter's blast.
Let him roar and let him rout,
We are armored for the bout.
How the logs are glowing, see!
Who sings louder, they or he?
Could the city be more gay?
Burn your bridges! Come away!

WHEN A FELLER'S ITCHIN' TO BE SPANKED

W'EN us fellers stomp around, makin' lots
    o' noise,
Gramma says, " There's certain times comes
    to little boys
W'en they need a shingle or the soft side of
    a plank; "
She says " we're a-itchin' for a right good
    spank."
      An' she says, " Now thes you wait,
      It's a-comin'—soon or late,
W'en a fellers itchin' fer a spank."

W'en a feller's out o' school, you know how he
    feels,
Gramma says we wriggle 'roun like a lot o'
    eels.
W'y it's like a man that's thes home from out
    o' jail.

Lyrics of Sunshine and Shadow

What's the use o' scoldin' if we pull Tray's
  tail?
    Gramma says, tho', " thes you wait,
    It's a-comin'—soon or late,
You'se the boys that's itchin' to be spanked."

Cats is funny creatures an' I like to make 'em
  yowl,
Gramma alwus looks at me with a awful scowl
An' she says, " Young gentlemen, mamma
  should be thanked
Ef you'd get your knickerbockers right well
  spanked."
    An' she says, " Now thes you wait,
    It's a-comin'—soon or late,"
W'en a feller's itchin' to be spanked.

Ef you fin' the days is gettin' awful hot
  in school
An' you know a swimmin' place where it's nice
  and cool,
Er you know a cat-fish hole brimmin' full o'
  fish,
Whose a-goin' to set around school and wish?

'Tain't no use to hide your bait,
It's a-comin'—soon or late,
W'en a feller's itchin' to be spanked.

Ol' folks know most ever'thing 'bout the
world, I guess,
Gramma does, we wish she knowed thes a
little less,
But I alwus kind o' think it 'ud be as well
Ef they wouldn't alwus have to up an' tell;
We kids wish 'at they'd thes wait,
It's a-comin'—soon or late,
W'en a feller's itchin' to be spanked.

THE RIVER OF RUIN

ALONG by the river of ruin
They dally—the thoughtless ones,
They dance and they dream
By the side of the stream,
As long as the river runs.

Lyrics of Sunshine and Shadow

It seems all so pleasant and cheery—
No thought of the morrow is theirs,
And their faces are bright
With the sun of delight,
And they dream of no night-brooding
    cares.

The women wear garlanded tresses,
The men have rings on their hands,
And they sing in their glee,
For they think they are free—
They that know not the treacherous sands.

Ah, but this be a venturesome journey,
Forever those sands are ashrift,
And a step to one side
Means a grasp of the tide,
And the current is fearful and swift.

For once in the river of ruin,
What boots it, to do or to dare,
For down we must go
In the turbulent flow,
To the desolate sea of Despair.

TO HER

YOUR presence like a benison to me
    Wakes my sick soul to dreamful
      ecstasy,
I fancy that some old Arabian night
Saw you my houri and my heart's delight.

And wandering forth beneath the passionate
    moon,
    Your love-strung zither and my soul in
      tune,
We knew the joy, the haunting of the pain
    That like a flame thrills through me now
      again.

To-night we sit where sweet the spice winds
    blow,
    A wind the northland lacks and ne'er shall
      know,
With clasped hands and spirits all aglow
    As in Arabia in the long ago.

A LOVE LETTER

OH, I des received a letter f'om de sweetest
little gal;
    Oh, my; oh, my.
She's my lovely little sweetheart an' her name
is Sal:
    Oh, my; oh, my.

She writes me dat she loves me an' she loves
me true,
  She wonders ef I'll tell huh dat I loves
huh, too;
An' my heaht's so full o' music dat I do'
know what to do;
    Oh, my; oh, my.

I got a man to read it an' he read it fine;
    Oh, my; oh, my.
Dey ain' no use denying dat her love is mine;
    Oh, my; oh, my.

Lyrics of Sunshine and Shadow

But hyeah's de t'ing dat's puttin' me in such
a awful plight,
I t'ink of huh at mornin' an' I dream of huh
at night;
But how's I gwine to cou't huh w'en I do'
know how to write?
    Oh, my; oh, my.

My heaht is bubblin' ovah wid de t'ings I
want to say;
    Oh, my; oh, my.
An' dey's lots of folks to copy what I tell 'em
fu' de pay;
    Oh, my; oh, my.
But dey's t'ings dat I's a-t'inkin' dat is only
fu' huh ears,
An' I couldn't lu'n to write 'em ef I took a
dozen years;
So to go down daih an' tell huh is de only
way, it 'pears;
    Oh, my; oh, my.

Lyrics of Sunshine and Shadow

AFTER MANY DAYS

I'VE always been a faithful man
   An' tried to live for duty,
But the stringent mode of life
   Has somewhat lost its beauty.

The story of the generous bread
   He sent upon the waters,
Which after many days returns
   To trusting sons and daughters,

Had oft impressed me, so I want
   My soul influenced by it,
And bought a loaf of bread and sought
   A stream where I could try it.

I cast my bread upon the waves
   And fancied then to await it;
It had not floated far away
   When a fish came up and ate it.

Lyrics of Sunshine and Shadow

And if I want both fish and bread,
    And surely both I'm wanting,
About the only way I see
    Is for me to go fishing.

LIZA MAY

LITTLE brown face full of smiles,
    And a baby's guileless wiles,
        Liza May, Liza May.

Eyes a-peeping thro' the fence
With an interest intense,
        Liza May.

Ah, the gate is just ajar,
And the meadow is not far,
        Liza May, Liza May.

And the road feels very sweet,
To your little toddling feet,
        Liza May.

Lyrics of Sunshine and Shadow

Ah, you roguish runaway,
What will toiling mother say,
          Liza May, Liza May?

What care you who smile to greet
Everyone you chance to meet,
          Liza May?

Soft the mill-race sings its song,
Just a little way along,
          Liza May, Liza May.

But the song is full of guile,
Turn, ah turn, your steps the while,
          Liza May.

You have caught the gleam and glow
Where the darkling waters flow,
          Liza May, Liza May.

Flash of ripple, bend of bough,
Where are all the angels now?
          Liza May.

Lyrics of Sunshine and Shadow

Now a mother's eyes intense
Gazing o'er a shabby fence,
>> Liza May, Liza May.

Then a mother's anguished face
Peering all around the place,
>> Liza May.

Hear the agonizing call
For a mother's all in all,
>> Liza May, Liza May.

Hear a mother's maddened prayer
To the calm unanswering air,
>> Liza May.

What's become of—Liza May?
What has darkened all the day?
>> Liza May, Liza May.

Ask the waters dark and fleet,
If they know the smiling, sweet
>> Liza May.

Lyrics of Sunshine and Shadow

Call her, call her as you will,
On the meadow, on the hill,
        Liza May, Liza May.

Through the brush or beaten track
Echo only gives you back,
        Liza May.

Ah, but you were loving—sweet,
On your little toddling feet,
        Liza May, Liza May.

But through all the coming years,
Must a mother breathe with tears,
        Liza May.

THE MASTERS

OH, who is the Lord of the land of life,
    When hotly goes the fray?
When, fierce we smile in the midst of strife
    Then whom shall we obey?

Lyrics of Sunshine and Shadow

Oh, Love is the Lord of the land of life
  Who holds a monarch's sway;
He wends with wish of maid and wife,
  And him you must obey.

Then who is the Lord of the land of life,
  At setting of the sun?
Whose word shall sway when Peace is rife
  And all the fray is done?

Then Death is the Lord of the land of life,
  When your hot race is run.
Meet then his scythe and pruning-knife
  When the fray is lost or won.

TROUBLE IN DE KITCHEN

DEY was oncet a awful quoil 'twixt de
    skillet an' de pot;
De pot was des a-bilin' an' de skillet sho'
  was hot.

Dey slurred each othah's colah an' dey called
each othah names,
W'ile de coal-oil can des gu-gled, po'in oil
erpon de flames.

De pot, hit called de skillet des a flat, disfig-
gered t'ing,
An' de skillet 'plied dat all de pot could do
was set an' sing,
An' he 'lowed dat dey was 'lusions dat he
wouldn't stoop to mek
'Case he reckernize his juty, an' he had too
much at steak.

Well, at dis de pot biled ovah, case his tempah
gittin' highah,
An' de skillet got to sputterin', den de fat
was in de fiah.
Mistah fiah lay daih smokin' an' a-t'inkin'
to hisse'f,
W'ile de peppah-box us nudgin' of de gingah
on de she'f.

99

Den dey all des lef' hit to 'im, 'bout de trouble
an' de talk;
An' howevah he decided, w'y dey bofe 'u'd
walk de chalk;
But de fiah uz so 'sgusted how dey quoil an'
dey shout
Dat he cooled 'em off, I reckon, w'en he
puffed an' des went out.

THE QUILTING

DOLLY sits a-quilting by her mother,
stitch by stich,
Gracious, how my pulses throb, how my
fingers itch,
While I note her dainty waist and her slender
hand,
As she matches this and that, she stitches
strand by strand.
And I long to tell her Life's a quilt and I'm
a patch;
Love will do the stitching if she'll only be my
match.

PARTED

SHE wrapped her soul in a lace of lies,
  With a prime deceit to pin it;
And I thought I was gaining a fearsome prize,
  So I staked my soul to win it.

We wed and parted on her complaint,
  And both were a bit of barter,
Tho' I'll confess that I'm no saint,
  I'll swear that she's no martyr.

FOREVER

I HAD not known before
  Forever was so long a word.
The slow stroke of the clock of time
  I had not heard.

'Tis hard to learn so late;
　　It seems no sad heart really learns,
But hopes and trusts and doubts and
　　　　fears,
　　And bleeds and burns.

The night is not all dark,
　　Nor is the day all it seems,
But each may bring me this relief—
　　My dreams and dreams.

I had not known before
　　That Never was so sad a word,
So wrap me in forgetfulness—
　　I have not heard.

CHRISTMAS

STEP wid de banjo an' glide wid de fiddle,
　　Dis ain' no time fu' to pottah an' piddle;
Fu' Christmas is comin', it's right on de way,
　　An' dey's houahs to dance 'fo' de break o'
　　de day.

Lyrics of Sunshine and Shadow

What if de win' is taihin' an' whistlin'?
  Look at dat fiah how hit's spittin' an'
    bristlin'!
Heat in de ashes an' heat in de cindahs,
  Ol' mistah Fros' kin des look thoo de
    windahs.

Heat up de toddy an' pas' de wa'm glasses,
  Don' stop to shivah at blowin's an' blas'es,
Keep on de kittle an' keep it a-hummin',
  Eat all an' drink all, dey's lots mo' a-comin'.
Look hyeah, Maria, don't open dat oven,
  Want all dese people a-pushin' an' shovin'?

Res' f'om de dance? Yes, you done cotch
    dat odah,
  Mammy done cotch it, an' law! hit nigh
    flo'd huh;
'Possum is monst'ous fu' mekin' folks fin' it!
  Come, draw yo' cheers up, I's sho' I do'
    min' it.

Eat up dem critters, you men folks an'
    wimmens,
  'Possums ain' skace w'en dey's lots o'
    pu'simmons.

ROSES AND PEARLS

YOUR spoken words are roses fine and
    sweet,
The songs you sing are perfect pearls of
    sound.
How lavish nature is about your feet,
To scatter flowers and jewels both around.

Blushing the stream of petal beauty flows,
Softly the white strings trickle down and
    shine.
Oh! speak to me, my love, I crave a rose.
Sing me a song, for I would pearls were mine.

RAIN-SONGS

THE rain streams down like harp-strings
    from the sky;
The wind, that world-old harpist, sitteth by;
And ever as he sings his low refrain,
    He plays upon the harp-strings of the rain.

A LOST DREAM

AH, I have changed, I do not know
    Why lonely hours affect me so.
In days of yore, this were not wont,
No loneliness my soul could daunt.

For me too serious for my age,
The weighty tome of hoary sage,
Until with puzzled heart astir,
One God-giv'n night, I dreamed of her.

Lyrics of Sunshine and Shadow

I loved no woman, hardly knew
More of the sex that strong men woo
Than cloistered monk within his cell;
But now the dream is lost, and hell

Holds me her captive tight and fast
Who prays and struggles for the past.
No living maid has charmed my eyes,
But now, my soul is wonder-wise.

For I have dreamed of her and seen
Her red-brown tresses, ruddy sheen,
Have known her sweetness, lip to lip,
The joy of her companionship.

When days were bleak and winds were rude,
She shared my smiling solitude,
And all the bare hills walked with me
To hearken winter's melody.

And when the spring came o'er the land
We fared together hand in hand
Beneath the linden's leafy screen
That waved above us faintly green.

Lyrics of Sunshine and Shadow

In summer, by the river-side,
Our souls were kindred with the tide
That floated onward to the sea
As we swept toward Eternity.

The bird's call and the water's drone
Were all for us and us alone.
The water-fall that sang all night
Was her companion, my delight,

And e'en the squirrel, as he sped
Along the branches overhead,
Half kindly and half envious,
Would chatter at the joy of us.

'Twas but a dream, her face, her hair,
The spring-time sweet, the winter bare,
The summer when the woods we ranged,—
'Twas but a dream, but all is changed.

Yes, all is changed and all has fled,
The dream is broken, shattered, dead.
And yet, sometimes, I pray to know
How just a dream could hold me so.

A SONG

ON a summer's day as I sat by a stream,
 A dainty maid came by,
And she blessed my sight like a rosy dream,
 And left me there to sigh, to sigh,
 And left me there to sigh, to sigh.

On another day as I sat by the stream,
 This maiden paused a while,
Then I made me bold as I told my dream,
 She heard it with a smile, a smile,
 She heard it with a smile, a smile.

Oh, the months have fled and the autumn's
 red,
 The maid no more goes by;
For my dream came true and the maid I wed,
 And now no more I sigh, I sigh,
 And now no more I sigh.

Lyrics of Sunshine and Shadow

A SONG

THOU art the soul of a summer's day,
   Thou art the breath of the rose.
  But the summer is fled
  And the rose is dead
Where are they gone, who knows, who knows?

Thou art the blood of my heart o' hearts,
Thou art my soul's repose,
  But my heart grows numb
  And my soul is dumb
Where art thou, love, who knows, who knows?

Thou art the hope of my after years—
Sun for my winter snows
  But the years go by
  'Neath a clouded sky.
Where shall we meet, who knows, who knows?